To my childhood companion,
my confidante, my forever friend . . .
my sister,_____
From,_____

Editor: Megan Langford
Art Director: Kevin Swanson
Designer: Sarah Smitka — The Pink Pear Design Company
Production Artist: Dan Horton

ISBN: 978-1-59530-245-8

BOK4365

Printed and bound in China

My Sister, My Friend

By Katherine Bontrager

GIFT BOOKS
from Hallmark

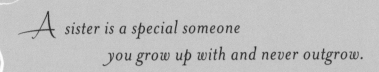

A sister is a special someone
you grow up with and never outgrow.

I'm so glad I got to grow up with you.
My earliest memory of us is:

_____

_____

_____

_____

We were gorgeous from the beginning, don't you think?

attach photo here

$\mathcal{W}$e have more nicknames for each other
than we can count, but my favorite is:

_____

Some family stories *never* get old!
Do you remember the time when:

_____

_____

_____

_____

$\mathcal{M}$y favorite times with you are when we:

- ○ talk on the phone
- ○ just hang out
- ○ grab a drink
- ○ reminisce about old times
- ○ go shopping
- ○ have dinner
- ○ _____
- ○ _____

If I could capture one day with you
and enjoy it over and over, it would be the day we:

_____

_____

_____

_____

No one can gently guide
or smack some sense into you quite like a sister.
The most important thing you taught me was:

_____

_____

_____

_____

With a sister,
     you'll never be in doubt about whether
you are over-accessorized, need a haircut,
          or have something in your teeth.

Family faces are magic mirrors.
Looking at people who belong to us,
we see the past, present, and future.
We make discoveries about ourselves.

—GAIL LUMET BUCKLEY

You keep me:
- ◯ sane
- ◯ honest
- ◯ laughing
- ◯ on my toes
- ◯ centered
- ◯ curious
- ◯ stylish
- ◯ in-the-know
- ◯ _____
- ◯ _____
- ◯ all of the above

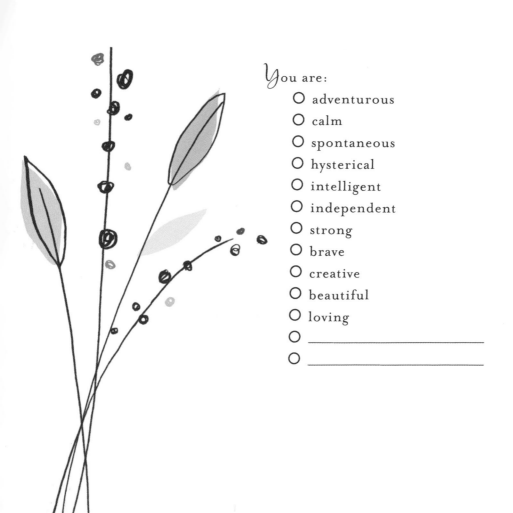

You are:
- O adventurous
- O calm
- O spontaneous
- O hysterical
- O intelligent
- O independent
- O strong
- O brave
- O creative
- O beautiful
- O loving
- O _____
- O _____

But of all your amazing qualities, my favorite is:

_____

_____

_____

_____

When I look back
on my favorite memories,
I find you there,
a part of every one.

I'm still extremely grateful for the time you:

_____

_____

_____

_____

If I made a CD of songs from our childhood,
here are a few I'd include:

_____

_____

_____

_____

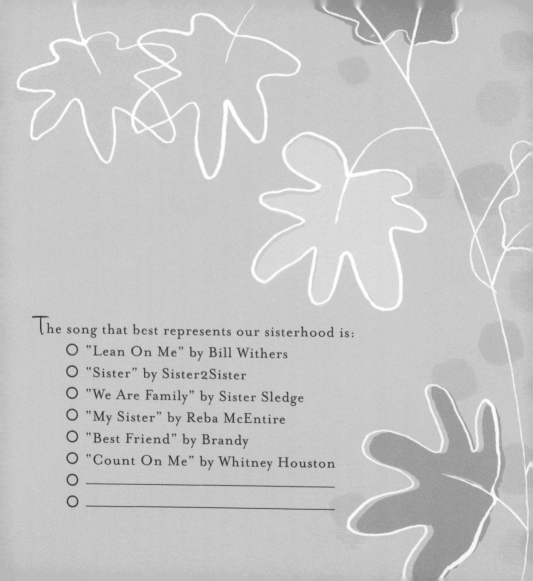

The song that best represents our sisterhood is:

- ○ "Lean On Me" by Bill Withers
- ○ "Sister" by Sister2Sister
- ○ "We Are Family" by Sister Sledge
- ○ "My Sister" by Reba McEntire
- ○ "Best Friend" by Brandy
- ○ "Count On Me" by Whitney Houston
- ○ _____
- ○ _____

Growing up, we had the most fun together when we:

_____

_____

_____

_____

$\mathcal{N}$ow that we're grown up,
we have an even better time together.
Wouldn't it be great if we:

_____

_____

_____

_____

If Hollywood made a movie about you,
the title would be:

_____

This is who would star as you:

_____

This is who would star as your beautiful,
loving sister (that's me!):

_____

The film would be a:

- O slapstick comedy
- O serious drama
- O wild action-adventure film
- O melodramatic musical
- O cartoon
- O _____

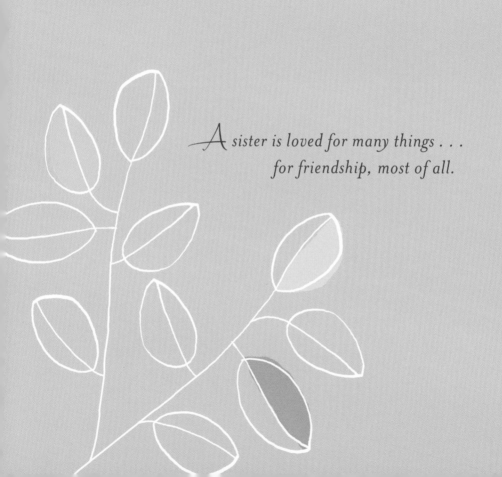

A sister is loved for many things . . .
for friendship, most of all.

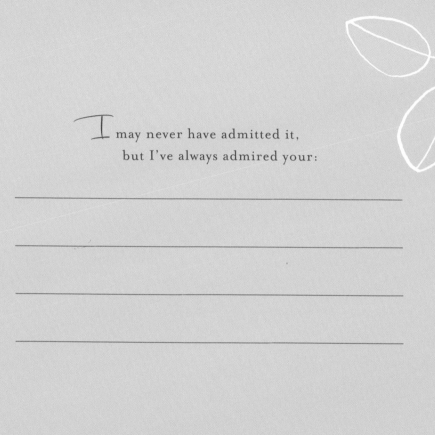

I may never have admitted it,
but I've always admired your:

_____

_____

_____

_____

$\mathcal{W}$ithout you, I never would have:

_____

_____

_____

_____

You've given me some incredible gifts.
One of my favorites was:

_____

_____

_____

_____

If we could escape for a few weeks,
we should definitely vacation in:

_____

_____

_____

_____

(And by the way—what's stopping us?!)

Spending time with you is:

○ memorable

○ always an adventure

○ the best kind of therapy

○ effortless and endlessly comfortable

○ marked by laughter and smart-aleck comments

○ always a treat

○ good for my soul

○ _____

○ _____

With your love and support, I know I can make it through anything. You were really there for me when:

_____

_____

_____

_____

You know when to stay silent,
 when to humor me, and when to call it like it is.
You've got that sneaky sister telepathy thing going on—
 somehow saying exactly what I need to hear . . .
 and sensing when I could use a smile.

You have been my:
- O cheerleader
- O kindest critic
- O therapist
- O sparring partner
- O personal shopper
- O oldest and dearest friend
- O partner in crime
- O voice of reason
- O guardian angel
- O _____
- O all of the above

Thank you for inspiring me to:

_____

_____

_____

_____

A look, a nod, a roll of the eyes—
    How is it that you can tell me
    all I need to know without saying a word?

Here are some quirky things I love about you:

_____

_____

_____

_____

$\mathcal{Y}$ou'd probably describe our relationship as:

_____

_____

_____

_____

Here's how I describe our relationship:

_____

_____

_____

_____

Remember this look?

attach photo here

Wow! I'm really glad we outgrew *that*.

Whether it involved gum, dye, or tweezers,
   behind every set of sisters is a hair-related tragedy
   that lives on in family legend.

A girl I knew back when.
A woman I've come to admire.
A friend who's always there . . .
A sister I'll always love.

I may not have told you at the time,
but I was so incredibly proud when you:

_____

_____

_____

_____

$\mathcal{A}$ story about us I never get tired of telling is:

_____

_____

_____

_____

The craziest stunt we ever pulled was:

_____

_____

_____

_____

Day by day, year by year,
I realize "sister"
is just another word for "friend."
Not just any friend,
but the most supportive,
intuitive, funny, amazingly generous,
true kind of friend.

When I brag about you, this is what I tell people:

_____

_____

_____

_____

You always make me laugh when you:

_____

_____

_____

_____

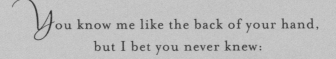

$\mathcal{Y}$ou know me like the back of your hand,
but I bet you never knew:

_____

_____

_____

_____

*I don't have to explain
anything to my sister . . .
She's one of the few people
who can read my heart.*

I love it when you:

- O call me to chat about nothing
- O give me one of your great hugs
- O let me vent my frustrations
- O laugh at my jokes
- O keep my secrets
- O seem to know exactly what I'm thinking
- O _____
- O _____

We survived all the
"I'm telling Mom's!"
and hissy fits
and came out best friends.
It turns out that shared memories,
pacts and promises,
and good, old-fashioned love
mattered more
than all that other stuff.

Even if you weren't my sister, you'd still be
one of my closest friends because:

_____

_____

_____

_____

Thanks for sharing your:

- ○ purse
- ○ shoes
- ○ little black dress
- ○ make-up tips
- ○ lawyer's phone number
- ○ _____
- ○ _____

*C*onfession time:

Even though you didn't want me to, I:

_____

_____

_____

_____

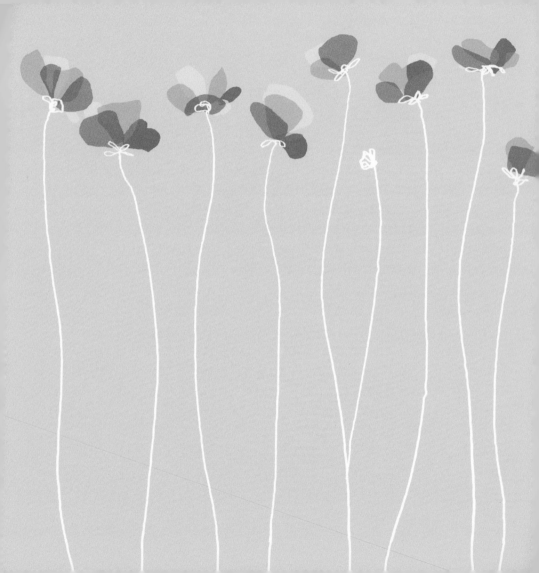

A sister is a special friend
who's there to share with you
and care about you
at all stages of life . . .
And to understand
in ways that no one else ever could.

If I had one wish for you, it would be:

_____

_____

_____

_____

Sisters share the past,
support each other in the here and now,
and help dream of what will come.

Together we've learned
    some of life's sweetest lessons . . .
how to live and love well . . .
        the importance of family . . .
    what it means to have and be a friend.

$\mathcal{A}$ family tradition I hope we continue is:

_____

_____

_____

_____

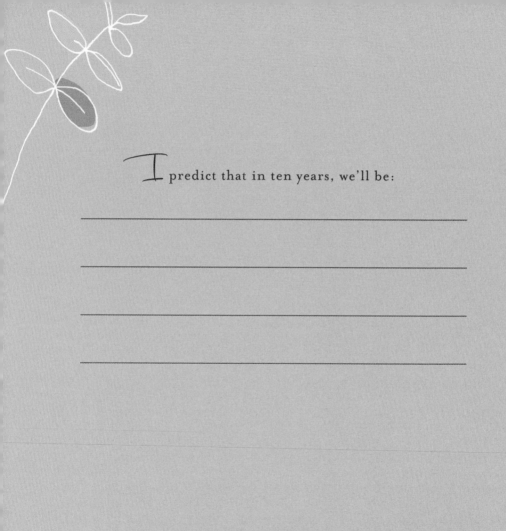

I predict that in ten years, we'll be:

_____

_____

_____

_____

I hope that when we're both old and gray, you'll look back on our relationship and say:

_____

_____

_____

_____

Still gorgeous. No question.

attach photo here

Time goes by.
The world changes.
We change.
But there's one thing you can count on . . .
love, especially family love,
and the love of your sister.
There's a link between us that will never break,
even if it's been stretched a time or two.
We've been through so much together;
we have so much in common.
I'll never stop caring about you,
worrying about you, wanting the best for you.
That can never change.
That's what love and friendship is all about.
That's what a sister is for.

$\mathcal{I}f$ you and your sister enjoyed this book
or it has touched your life in some way,
we would love to hear from you.

Please send your comments to:
Hallmark Book Feedback
P.O. Box 419034
Mail Drop 215
Kansas City, MO 64141

Or e-mail us at:
booknotes@hallmark.com